# *TIPPING POINT*

By

## D. E. Ritterbusch

**For Patricia**

*who always wanted*
*a witch doctor,*
*a bush pilot, a poet,*
*and does not realize*
*she got the worst of the lot.*

# ACKNOWLEDGMENTS

EARTH'S DAUGHTERS: *Full Measure*

FAR FROM THE TEMPLE OF HEAVEN: *Kandinsky and Me, The Bridge, The Lingering Flavor of Rice*

GEMINI MAGAZINE: *Expiation*

GREAT RIVER REVIEW: *Some Things; Sphagnum*

KUDZU PRESS: *A Flittering Cosmology; Broken Glass*

LAKE SUPERIOR STATE UNIVERSITY LITERARY REVIEW: *Wind Shear*

NEW VERSE NEWS: *Interior*

ONE TRICK PONY: *What the Light Would Say*

ROCKHURST REVIEW: *Odysseus*

SMALLER THAN GOD: *Acolytes; Landlord Lamentations*

THE BOILER: A JOURNAL OF NEW LITERATURE: *Tipping Point*

WAR, LITERATURE & THE ARTS: *Assyrian Lament*

WISCONSIN ACADEMY REVIEW: *The Quarry*

BODY LANGUAGE: *Green Tea*

Ted Kooser republished *Green Tea* in his national newspaper column AMERICAN LIFE IN POETRY. *Green Tea* was read on National Public Radio, THE WRITER'S ALMANAC, by Garrison Keillor and was also part of a New Zealand collaboration between poets and artists in *When North Meets South*.

Grateful thanks is given to the editors of the publications wherein this work was previously published.

Cover Art by Jane Irish:  Detail from Sông Hu'o'ng, 2013, egg tempera on canvas, 94 inches x 20 feet.

# Contents

# SOME THINGS

Some things stay forever,
some things last the lifespan
of a mayfly, iridescent
for a moment, even less

The plastic grocery bag
hanging in a tree
two houses down
has been there, flying in the wind
like a wounded kite
for two long winters, even more

It shows no sign of leaving

And the lures, spinner baits
and jointed minnows wrapped
around a wire—fishermen
cast them from an iron bridge;
its rusted scale
          flickers
     to the water below

The lures tangle and twist;
a hard retrieve whips them tight,
line reluctantly cut

They serve as warning for those who follow

Yet every fall there's more,
dry wind

　　　whipping
　　spoons and flutter blades,
a caution for the birds

A walk under the wires
raises a covey of burrs;
they grab pant legs and socks,
refuse to come off
even in the wash

It's the same everywhere—
along the Mekong, plastic bags
bring boats to a dead stop;
their props twist tighter
and tighter, plastic
hard to cut, unwilling to let go

We drift in wakes
of other boats, pass a temple
in disrepair, a monument to war
in the distance.  I wave
to a small boy fishing
while his mother washes clothes
in the river.  He smiles
when I wave to him again.

Cutting done, our boatman tosses
shreds of plastic back to the water—
fish too small to keep—he pulls
the recoil starter; the engine
chuffs alive

Acknowledging this timeless
stoppage, a moment of reflection
flying in a neighbor's tree,
lures caught and spinning on a wire,
a prop stopped, like memory—

In water and air
some things hold
the heart, time, the river
that passes with a current
of understanding, a ballet
of prickliness that sticks
and stays beyond the limits
of our cast off days

# ODYSSEUS

I was on my way
to see you
when an old friend
stopped me
on the street,
reminded me
of something,
of some other life,
and too,
I was distracted
by a pale flower
growing in an uneven crack
in the pavement
as I looked down
thinking
of something to say,
and one idea
led to the next
so I went back
retracing the steps
I'd taken
and found someone
more like you
than you yourself
when I got home.
How wondrous
to relive one's journey
and find all
one set out to find

right there
in a place
once left behind.

# THE LINGERING FLAVOR OF RICE

She cooked rice for breakfast,
awakened to air conditioned air
stale from a long night in a closed room,
windows shut against the humid dark.
Her back narrowed to her small waist
as she bent over the rice;
her hair caught the light of morning.

It was another time, another country,
and the pleasures were so new.

So please forgive me if I always
connect the fragrance of cooking rice
with making love, the taste
always the same, the lingering pleasure.

Love is always the same, familiar
as a bowl of rice, and yet one kiss
is not the same as any other,
differences greater than with grains
of rice. Perhaps it's foolish
to make such connections, to
continue year after year with the same
associative remembrance.

You will record things differently,
each to each.

I'll entertain another possibility:
when days linger into years,
when they stick together
like a clump of rice
in the white light of an afternoon,
time might recall
not the white of the rice, her slim back,
her slender arms reaching for salt
but something else entirely, an orange
perhaps, the way she opened it
discovering its orange heart
as she offers—arm extended
like a priest's offering the sacrament
of orange—a dripping segment,
the fragrance of orange
opening each morning
always and even now as I write
of the slender arms, the gentle hands of rice.

# A FLITTERING COSMOLOGY

A crashed dragonfly beats
        the still water of this lake
            at noon, the sun high
the water dead flat except
        for the rippled thrash
            of four wings unable to lift—
a gift to bass and northern pike.
        My canoe glides by;
            I scoop the dragonfly,
exhausted, from the water, a smooth
        cupping of my hand beneath
            brought up into that most familiar
element of flight.  He rests
        on my index finger, sunlight
            quickly drying his wings.
His head bends down, touches my finger
        once, twice, again
            as if a kiss of thanks:
you and I know that's nonsense—
        anthropomorphizing an insect—
            and yet we've made the old gods guilty
of our most venial sins; it is not error
        to think of seamless patterns,
            life forms nascent and ancient linked.
More likely he thought my finger
        to be food, sustenance, replenishment—
            god knows what dragonflies will eat.
But I prefer another explanation:
        both of us here but briefly,

a chance meeting, the day balanced
on a still point; it could all go
either way, spilling into the drink.
Perhaps, in that wild dimension
physicists call Imaginary Time, some strange
and wondrous change
will be effected—
an altered past
re-coursing everything: our dragonfly
launches into the quiet
sun, is lost against the tree line,
all of us replenished,
so resplendently sustained.

# PREDICTIONS

*Poetry and science are gifts*
*given to all of humanity.*
Freeman Dyson

I imagine poetry
to be an orchid
deep in its folds,
a long slender tube,
a champagne flute
fashioned with the most delicate
of petalled fabrics,
white as a wedding gown.

Knowing that great apes
would be offended,
Darwin studied orchids
the better to avoid
a fruitless war with God,
another foolish controversy—
as if God mattered to a flower.

And when Darwin's friend
shipped him a specimen
from Madagascar
Darwin studied
that orchid's shape,
its grand design,
and knew well
that somewhere

There must be
a pollinator
with a proboscis large enough,
long enough, to reach
the golden grains
nestled in a foot long nectary—
nature not usually given
to uselessness.

But Darwin never found it,
no botanist, no lepidopterist, ever recorded,
any insect—
neither butterfly nor moth—
with a penetrator
long enough to probe
the nectaries,
those slender filaments of green
tenuously attached.

No proof then
of Darwin's prognostication.

Predictions in poetry and science
run much the same,
the organic structure of a poem
means the poem
with unfounded predictability
ends far
from where it began.

And just so
that moth—
forty-five years after

Darwin predicted its existence—
was found in the wilds of Madagascar
and eighty-five years later,
more than a century and a quarter
after Darwin imagined
its inevitable presence

The moth, X. morganii praedicta,
was observed
dipping its long proboscis
into the slender, green tendrils,
the nectaries,
of A. sesquipedale, conjoining then
both poetry and science,
cross-pollinating
the world made beautiful
each coevolving to each,
moth to orchid, orchid to moth
in immeasurable grace.

# TAKING THOREAU'S ADVICE TO AVOID THE NEWS

> Blessed are they who never read
> a newspaper . . . .
>
> H.D. Thoreau

Rustication has not worked
intrusions constant though sequestered
steeled away in patterned shade;
loss and regret still seek this cloister out

Occultation does not serve either
and putting the senses to sleep
means a parade of tabloid dreams
again marches to waking

Nightmare upon shameful nightmare,
one wrong after another springing
to life, might as well stay awake
in a dolorous state, almost admiring

A stray cat on the porch, that abject look
in its eyes, waiting to be fed, but
wishing all this begging could be done with—
no one truly believes in the psalm of survival

An easy out.  Relinquishing pleasure
and equivalent retribution, as if
predestination were not ordained:
a monk's white robe flutters like a flag

Even the godless await another coming

# ACOLYTES

On Sunday we help each other
with our Lutheran robes, joke about drinking
the communion wine
breathing red as blood
next to wafers on the silver tray.
And this week is the hard one—
fresh candles high above the altar:
it would be weeks before they'd burn down
low enough to light, easy, within reach,
and so we stand holding the flame
far above our heads, guessing at the wick,
feel that palpable Christian impatience
in faces of the congregation; my brow sweats
amid the stares, but you get lucky,
and the low flame holds.
Relieved, you wait for me as stern church fathers
confirm my uselessness to God.  And God,
what must he think of my inability even to light
this simple ivory candle tipped with gold?
All my life now I feel God's impatient stare:
I get so little right, and never the first time
through, everything, always, just beyond reach
a candle's length away.

# THE QUARRY

*No Trespassing* signs
aren't much of a deterrent
when you're seventeen
and the water is the deepest
blue-green you've ever seen—
promise of cool water
after dark, a forbidden swim
into unmarked dangers,
no line of floats, no lifeguard,
just the quiet call of crickets
and a few stars charting a safer course.
It is a tradition taking off our clothes,
diving in, swimming to the rock ledge
across the quarry where we could rest,
catching our breath, stilling the heart
to tell stories, brag of girlfriends,
pronounce our futures, rag on
teachers for their silly rules.

And on that night, late,
when even our friends were fast asleep,
almost on a dare you and I
parked down the road,
snuck over the fence,
walked to the water
to watch the still moon float.
My arm around your shoulders
slipped to your waist, a touch
among the crickets, night birds calling,

quarry stone still warm
from the lengthening sun.
The moon rode on the silken water
as we kissed, as we broke
apart to feel the embarrassed thrill
of being nude.  We jumped in,
the water deep and cool as a kiss,
the touch of your wet arms, your back,
treading the deep soul of the night.
And we swam, breaking the moon
into small pieces of light and water,
and when we crawled back out
your arms shivered, your shoulders,
as much from my kiss as from
the late night chill.

What could have happened
in all these years
to break that spell, to lose everything
the water dreamed?

# SENSIBILIIA COMMUNIA

We have before us an easy
proposition: *common sensibles*
are simple to discern—a child
affirms the world when fire trucks,
race red down his familiar street.
And mainly we stay there,
*proper sensibles* added
to the repertoire.  But there is more—
the recollection of a scent lived
years before, jasmine in a carafe
of water on the other side of the world.
The room filled with its perfume,
green geckos climbing overhead
intoxicated, why else hang upside
down in such a scent? Yet consider
another proposition: Love in a rainy season
may be considered an *uncommon sensible*
or maybe there is no sense
other than sensation that stays
long after the bed sheets cool and dry,
a lingering scent across the shoulders
of the world, recalled every time it rains.

# SPHAGNUM

Tamarack and black spruce
edge this bog—stunted
by acid-black water,
sphagnum spongy
and cool to the touch—a foot down
colder than a block of ice
in summer.  I slip the canoe
past an old beaver lodge,
watch crayfish scatter,
test the light springy moss
with a tentative step,
then walk to a rise of surer ground.
I hold a fistful of the old dressing
in my hand, recall its use
by surgeons in the First
World War—three times the absorbency
of cotton, three times the speed
at soaking blood, slightly acidic,
a natural antibiotic
helping the wounded to heal,
to prevent death by infection.
It is the light green coolness I feel
when I compress it in my hand,
another war in another time
as far removed as the burning
of compressed blocks of peat, dried
and fired for warmth for thousands
of years of war and peace and the forgetting
that dissipates like the heat,
like tracks of a crayfish
scuttling for cover.

# THE BRIDGE

## I

Early evening between
two middle spans
an old Buick shifts to the outside lane
and stops—cars brake and swerve,
snake around that Riviera
rusted, dented, angled across the lane—
a man unbuckles
and slides out, moves to the rail,
leans over, looks to the water below
and lifts a leg over the rusted steel
as if mounting the Schwinn
he rode as a young boy.
He moves deftly to another rail,
straddles it for a moment
the way he crossed over a fence
taking a short cut home after school.
He steps to a further beam, then another
and stands with the sun behind him
balanced on his toes, rocking
back and forth the way he stood
on the diving board that first time
so many years ago, everything
practice for the present moment,
horns honking with encouragement behind him.
There is no question
left unanswered
no answer left unquestioned.

His splash is soundless.
The fading sun rides barely discernible circles,
plays them until they subside to nothing,
water flat and gray as the bridge.

## II

But what if the questions
were all the wrong questions,
answers having nothing to do
with evening sun on the water;
what if all the essential parts,
or clues, or helpful household hints
were missing, what if he
overlooked everything—his wife's
hair streaming across the pillow
that first morning after the birth
of their son, the pumpkinseed
he pulled from a lake
with a bamboo pole, airplanes
he drew in grade school
when the teacher wasn't looking,
his Cub Scout uniform
covered with badges,
Monarch butterflies he caught
and released in his room: they flew
to the window, reaching for light.

## III

What if his wife turned away
as he brushed the hair from her face,
if he felt the sharp barb in his mouth,

and grew up hating to fly;
what if uniforms made him angry,
and there was never enough light?

### IV

What if we all got it wrong
crossing over the bridge
swerving and cursing,
honking our horns, raising
the middle finger in salute,
dropping a coin at the toll booth?

### V

What if no one gets it right
and this is the way it's supposed to be
every life lived in the dark,
every light, every mirrored reflection,
an illusion, liquid and elusive?

Even so, the sun warms our backs
in the middle of night,
in the middle of a bridge
whether we think it or not,
wind singing through the wire.

What if the car just stalled?

# SUNG DYNASTY VERSE

It is a morning to read
Chinese Court poetry,
few lines, few images
an underlayment of political intrigue

I learn little, preferring to stay
on the surface of the poems
heedless of the history, the metaphorical
and spiritual significance of kingfishers,
pomegranates, palace gates, the pulse of seasons

I prefer not to know
those flowers, gardens, mountains, clouds
mean more than themselves:
I want no meaning other than the simple
naming of things, their elemental experience

Perhaps I have grown tired
of orchestrating an exegesis,
an enlightened explication,

Preferring blossoms lilt in the change to evening,
a return, the same path going back,
passing, pausing, the seasons one by one

# A WARM DAY NEAR THE ONSET OF WINTER

So unexpected few of us venture out

Regret spins in the air reproaching the wind

I think I am somewhere else
as if the seasons cannot change,
remembrance of some wondrous evening
somewhere else I cannot recall

This is what the light does late in the day

This is the absence of birds, their call
to prayer, an absence of scripture
plotting the path.

I walk but a short distance past dusk,
then pause on a small bridge
overlooking a river bound by faith,
the river moving
with the flow of an old hymn

I watch it meld
into evening shadow; it vanishes

in a whisper of penitential grace

# INTERIOR

Two dogs bark back and forth, a common
interruption in summer, but this a cold
night in March, still a foot, maybe more, of snow
on the ground.  The traveler listens, stops thinking
for a moment, turns back to his book,
but nothing holds his attention.  Returned from
a long trip to the interior of a place
he had never been before, he
wants to reflect yet at the same time rid himself
of everything he'd seen: a man bit by a venomous snake
who just sat down and waited;
long worms white and thin as spaghetti
swimming like sea snakes in the drinking water;
bodies carved with machetes,
their limbs swelled in the sun like bratwurst;
and children living in the ruins
of a colonial mission, suspicion in their eyes
when any adult walked near.  These were all
things he'd known or heard of before, of course,
no matter where he traveled or when.  Field workers,
maimed and limbless because of mines, neglect, political
philosophy, it didn't matter.  Better to stay home
and read about the world, to let considered reflection
or a splendid forgetting get in the way,
like that small boy in the road
the convoy didn't brake for, because no one
stops for anything in that place.

# GOATFISH IN BLUE

It begins like all stories
of the goatfish, gilded
fins, scales of iridescent blue,
a pure wildness of color—imagine
a blue and silver thrashing on the deck,
its gills a scintillating red.

But in this version of the story,
its voice redolent with burnished gold,
it speaks candidly, persuasively,
with the old fisherman,
offers riches, glory, and fame:
he imagines them all, finds
nothing to entertain,
no value in a heavenly change;
he reads the deep line cuts in his hand,
feels his back weary
with the day's meager haul,
prefers his trawling routine.

He declines every offer, every appeal;
claims to reason don't work.
Upon its release, he won't even watch
that luminous glide beneath the waves—
the water indifferent,
his heart beating the same.

# EGRETS, HERONS, AND CRANES

An egret stands in the marsh grass,
looks warily across the span of water,
the open sky and field, bends down,
neck bowed, head disappeared in the long grass
and rises, a small fish or frog wriggling in its beak.
It is hard from here, this vantage point, to tell
just what is giving up its life to the crane.

Yes, of course it is a crane, even from here,
this distance, this shimmering light
of mortality; its neck is so much shorter.
I am sorry about the confusion,
so much error and in so much abundance.
Perhaps if I were closer I could tell,
but then, witness to the last convulsive
twitch before going limp, I'd be reminded:
something always dies so something else may live.

Our heron as symbol stands for a long
and generous life, so often found in Chinese
landscapes, the walls of Egypt, dynasty
after dynasty though the Bennu is long since
extinct, stands in our memory
of the first time we glimpse into time's
warped savagery, loss even more the loss
when one reflects.  And then there passes
a moment of regret, the association
unmistakable, lasting past the slow
flap of heavy wings, soon lost in the abiding sun.

# ASSIGNATION

Stopped at an intersection, the usual
long wait for the light to turn,
the arrow to appear, he gives
the man dressed in the usual garb—
pants, shirt, jacket all a camel-shit brown—
a dollar, *why,* he thinks, of all the stops,
all the men, all the cardboard signs
virtually unreadable, why this one a dollar?,
and he thinks of the last time, the last dollar
he gave as if some decent interval
had passed and he needed to give again, a dollar
lasting only so long, and he thought
of that bridge, the Danube, Buda and Pest
joined by a long walkway of women bent
in supplication, their hands stretched out
before them as they lie bowed to the steel
framework in what must be a painful
posture to hold, waiting for a coin to be placed
in the upturned palm, and he didn't give
freely enough, because so many,
because giving fatigue, because guilt at the plight
of another is easy to escape, a simple walk
over a bridge, a push of the accelerator
as the green light glows calling everyone
to move quickly because to stay, to look at
the man's face, the woman's hand,
is to deny the expansion of creation,
everything moving away at greater and greater speeds.

# WIND SHEAR

Someone, in a learned, scientific
journal, played a practical joke,
proposing a rigorous study of traffic
traveling across the continent,
suggesting wind patterns developed
in the continual rush of trucks
and cars from LA to New York and back
which affect the weather, perhaps causing
summer tornadoes in Kansas, high winds
along the shores of Maine.

High above those roads, in a 737,
I look out onto the clouds below,
patterns of dreamy movement
droning in my ear: in this reverie
of travel, my mind tries to make sense of it all
as it often does when I find a simple
but gnawing variance between what I see
and what I know.

               Without warning
the plane drops sharply,
hundreds of feet out of the air;
my seatbelt cuts into my sinking gut
as I'm pulled weightless out of my seat.
A moment later, stability regained
like a lost inheritance,
the Captain says, in his calming voice,
*We just got caught, for an instant,*

*behind another aircraft; jet wash*
*caused a bit of turbulence, but there's*
*nothing to worry about.*   There's
never anything to worry about;
we always land safely.  Tires
bump and screech; puffs of rubbery
smoke signal our return to earth.

It's almost a joke how safely we land;
nothing really affects anything else.
On a cold fall day I look up to the sky,
see long wedges of geese
flying south, auguries of whatever
we want things to be,
knowing the turbulence
of whatever has been lost
may safely be left behind
in the sheer force of these playful winds
signaling winter, or perhaps
a gentle rain closing down on the Maldives.

# ASSYRIAN LAMENT

From an Assyrian chamber pot
one can fabricate almost anything—
sunlight sparking on the sea, an awaking
to the crumpled breeze, a rough
rubbing of the beard while the woman
lying next assumes a grand and luxurious curve
arcing from shoulder to waist
and then the rise, her hip, her dimpled
derriere: he snuggles his beard
into a dimple, wakes her with a warm
devotional kiss.  The walls appear
as alabaster in this morning light,
the chamber pot is figured,
lovers entwined like a knot of snakes.
The lovers are always the same:
a thrall of carnal bliss while in the corner
a shield and spear.  After so much thrall
there is the call of scudding clouds,
movement other than her arched back;
he imagines the death masks that await,
welcomes the empty eyes of an iron god,
his own brimming with escape.

# AN ESSAY ON ZERO TOLERANCE

My daughter, barely three, is at the age of play,
and I'm at work teaching a night course,
trying to be human when the humanities
prove the least humane of all our academic disciplines.
I document our silly prevarications,
our penchant for error:  as Yogi Berra said
*We make too many wrong mistakes*—no matter
how many lessons we've been taught.
So when I return home from the university
I find she has a cast on her leg, a deep
fluorescent pink, as if color mitigates
the break.  Even today she still loves
fluorescent colors: backpack, running shoes
glowing in the dark.  Tibia fractured,
the doctor looks askance; it's the second
bone she's broken.  Examining X-rays he asks her
how it happened: I've been told the story,
how her mother told her not to jump
from the play set in the park onto the hard
playground surface, this in the days
before swing sets were removed by cautious
legislators, and recycled tires were ground into
a softer surface.  But she jumped anyway,
clowning, laughing, her knees locked, jumped despite
her mother's admonition, as we all do, as we did
to become who we are, separate, playing
apart from parents, from anyone
insisting otherwise, even our gods
created as reflections of ourselves:

Manjushri, god of wisdom, always warring
with the god of doing something dumb.
*I jumped stupid,* my daughter said,
admitting a fault, admitting the right
to do the wrong thing because so many rules
are foolish, and we have before us
so many fabled adults who misbehave, history
the record of that misbehavior.
So if there's a lesson here, it lies inside
that fluorescent cast, a break that teaches
we do wrong regardless, and who's to tell us
there's any other way to live, to learn,
to jump for joy, even if it is stupid.


*For Kerry*

# ORACLE

One works not to be desperate
yet one day melds into another
and not even a gold star,
barely a word of praise when the project's done;
*Good job* the boss says and his tone
is set; he'll say the same tonight:
*Good dog, that's a good dog*
and *Dinner was good tonight* to his wife,
in effect saying, *Good wife, that's a good wife*
though he wouldn't dare, and yet she knows
that's what he thinks and yet she doesn't care.
Only two more years until the children go
into that good world, to do good works.
Or not.  Better a faith not in good words
but those of a woman walking the streets
desperate to say something someone will
respond to, her hair mangled like her words,
and not even one thin dime because we cross
the street, pretend not to be desperate,
a hot gibberish spat from our good souls.

# LAMENTATION FOR MARTYRS

It must always be a warm day
branches withered and dry;
stones not frozen to the earth
but warm to the hand.

Eyes squinting, shaded by an upraised arm,
discern shadows of flame and stone
across parched rough colors of ground.

Life passes, quickly, like the shadow of a hawk
diving sharply into the trees.

Anlage, plerophory, uberrima fides,
rooted in the soul.

Take root or fly.

But imagine, suddenly, the sky turn white,
unclothed arms shiver, shoulders hunch-up
into the neck—no shadows, only the dull white
glaze of particles of sky tumbling down
to freeze the trembling root where it lies, to put out
the flames, freeze stones into the dirt where even
the hardest kick can't set them free.

Everyone, arms crossed in self-embrace, stumbling
against the wind, turns to go home.

An ecclesiolatry of white:
there are no martyrs in the snow.

# A WISDOM

Of many philosophies,
some gardens of truth,
all decaying as a peony blossom
in the heat, in shimmering waves
of rain tearing its petals apart.
Such are the vagaries
of any system of belief,
all mine for the asking.

But—as Heraclitus intoned—
all ways are the same way
and no truthful proposition
can stand for long—in heat,
in waves of rain, the years
beating it down, beating it down,
hail at the height
of summer.

# LANDLORD LAMENTATIONS

The tenant downstairs
says Carlos is in the Spanish Mafia.
They deal drugs and scrawl graffiti
under the bridge outside of town.
Even when she's home
the woman across the hall
double locks her door,
ignores what she hears, what she sees.
Carlos complains about the lack of heat,
leaves his windows open all winter
so the smoke, the smell of grass, will dissipate.
On the night before he skips
he pushes his girlfriend down the stairs-
a baluster breaks; the girl cries.
He tells her he has other girlfriends, many;
she must understand, as we all must,
finally, in the end.  I listen to stories
other tenants tell me,
imagine their lives, his life, what
it means to live like that.  If I understood
any of this I would be someone else,
someone in a different life; what would I learn,
what would I know?  I could repent
a life like that, and my repentance
would lift the sorrow of the world.
I clean the walls of his apartment, fill
chinks in the plaster, like bullet holes,
find the face of Jesus in a stain
bleeding down the walls.  Jesus is in tears;

we're both in tears.  We all want
the same thing: to look into the face of God
without shame, to earn eternal salvation, to get the rent
every month, always paid on time.

# KANDINSKY AND ME

Sculpture: *That's something you bump into when*
*you back up to look at a painting.*
—Barrett Newman

The gallery is small
given that the Kandinsky
I'm looking at is large,
too large for this room
and the track-lighting overhead
glares harshly off the paint
because the ceiling isn't high enough
so I back up to see the painting
more clearly with the proper perspective,
and I barely nudge a statue, Greek,
an antiquity that doesn't quite
belong in a room with Kandinsky and me.
So this security guard comes over,
touches my shoulder, says, *Don't*
*lean on the sculpture.*  I say, *I'm not leaning,*
*I'm backing up to look at the painting,*
and he says, *We have rules; you can't*
*touch the exhibit* and I say
*I'm not touching it, I'm not even*
*looking at it; I'm looking at the painting,*
and he says, *You won't think*
*your mouth is so smart*
*when I throw you out of here,*
and I say, *That's a fine thing*
*to consider, given that the gallery*

*is virtually empty and it's not like*
*this place is going berserk with*
*all the rich and famous patrons*
*crowding around.*  He says, *We*
*can do quite well without patrons*
*like you.* I say, *Kandinsky*
*had me in mind when he created*
*that painting which is far beyond*
*the rudimentary understanding of a security guard*
*who wouldn't know the difference*
*between a Renaissance painting*
*and a soup can—if it*
*weren't labeled as art.*  And besides
I say, *that statue is Greek; it's had*
*its nose broken, several times,*
*and its arms were cut off long ago*
*so it's not like there'd be any*
*real damage if it were to fall*
*while I'm looking at the Kandinsky*
*and not leaning on the Greek as you said*
*and how would you like your*
*nose to look like that?*
He puts both hands on my shoulders
shoves me past Miro, all his fantasy figures
staring, past DeChirico's ruins,
past a nude, I think, descending, past
one Bible story after another
until I'm outside, in a garden
surrounded by sculpture,
a large nude—Henry Moore I believe—
with full thighs, heavy breasts,
a body no one could break
in a gazillion years.  And I think

this isn't so bad as I look at it
from every angle, backing up
until I fall across a garden bench,
Victorian, ornamental iron,
filigree of peacocks and vines,
freshly labeled with an artistic sign
that reads BE CAREFUL FRESH PAINT.

# GREEN TEA

There is this tea
I have sometimes,
Pan Long Ying Hao,
so tightly curled
it looks like tiny roots
gnarled, a greenish-gray.
When it steeps, it opens
the way you woke this morning,
stretching, your hands behind
your head, back arched,
toes pointing, a smile steeped
in ceremony, a celebration,
the reaching of your arms.

# BROKEN GLASS

His movement was sure, sincere,
practiced, and yet it brushed against
a canister of tea, a glass container
solid and thick, holding an oily spiced tea
that would eat through a traditional tin,
one printed with bucolic scenes
of some idealized Chinese landscape,
and when it fell to the hardwood floor
it shattered in the predictable way
glass shatters, a patterned sparkle for days
of loose uncollected pieces:
just so, in a time long before,
his wife had stepped on a shard,
and believing herself merely superficially cut,
though a laceration that bled profusely
as if written in some bad crime fiction,
she redressed the wound
and complained that it did not heal
so he looked at it and found a piece that he teased
from her flesh like shrapnel from an old war wound,
and yet still she limped through the rest of that day
and the next though she refused further attention
because a bloody footprint reminded her
of an accident of her youth—a classmate had stepped
between parked cars after school and was hit,
the car not stopping for a block, pretending
as if nothing had happened, and the girl bled
so vividly, a chunk of headlight in her arm,
that no experience with everyday cuts

and scrapes could allay or diminish
its long term presence, and so it was only
with insistence that her foot was looked at again
and another splinter of glass was found
buried deeper than the first, and still he wondered
why in the sharp sting of every step
she refused further examination as if
the examination were more hurtful
than the glass itself, whereupon, with similar reflection,
a glance of the sun caught a multifaceted
piece as if some rough cut of a gemstone
appeared on a shelf of the kitchen cabinet
open at the time of the brusque, sure movement
of his hand as it brushed the canister,
as he reached in to police, a year later,
that perfect glistening reminder (working like a string
around a finger, a long scar that refuses to disappear)
a reminder of what is always there
because when one vessel is broken
and finally cleared of all evidence of its breaking,
another, with the same sureness of the hand,
will break and take its everlasting place

# PASSING

*—I love all things that pass . . .*
Siegfried Sassoon

I saw once a field of daffodils,
yellow near as far as I could see,
pleasure that returns but briefly
nestled in some spare and quiet time,
and that woman in a yellow dress,
one dance and I was smitten.
That word too has passed
among so many fleeting things:
the woman went on to other evenings,
the field was turned to pasture.
There is so little left that doesn't break
like an heirloom teacup dropped into a sink,
yet I recall green tea the morning after
that yellow strap slipped off her shoulder.

# AN IGNOMINIOUS EVENING

Mid autumn and rain sticks
fallen leaves to everything they touch

The air still holds the warmth
of summer

And there is that stillness
despite the rain
with so few leaves left on the trees

Does the family dog know
as it shakes rain from its musky fur
after its romp through backyards
its return to the back porch
splattering mud on your pants
dropping a bone at your feet?

At first you think it is the remains
of a possum that lived under your porch
a few years before, but a closer look
reveals it to be human, a wrist bone perhaps

You call the police; their red and blue lights
spin through the rain.  Isn't much
they can do they tell you,
but their flashlights comb the grass,
puddle light along a fence line,
bring neighbors to the yard

Same thing the next day; then nothing.
Lab analysis tells them little: you're not
informed.  There might be a thousand possibilities,
a thousand graves underfoot

It is a quiet interrogation:
the sky refuses to clear

No one believes the rain will end
despite the forecast, no one believes
any particular story about the wrist

It is a day to keep the dog inside

# TIPPING POINT

Once again
      the same wind
   bites and  claws
       at the trees
I welcome     its return
    as I wish its departure    happily
      leaving behind
     that stillness
       that slowing of the blood

On the ground     a rush of leaves
      a squirrel's nest    scattered
    a branch   fallen
        on the neighbor's car
   this     the only damage
         the only evidence
     of a natural violence
       a wizened insurrection

Each year I measure
    the quickening    the slowing
      that luminous   wing of air
       settling with a warm
    resonant voice    a monk's call
         to prayer

A tuft of moon    brushes the trees
   a scent of wood burning
      curls around the house
   now   if only  the war would end

if the terrain of reason
would give way
and the soft reflected light
would linger
as in another country
living   a geography of silence
wordless        as a feral child
and similarly    content

# WHAT THE LIGHT WOULD SAY

In the language of the Dakota
*um pa o wasta we*
means *beautiful daybreak woman.*
I imagine a Dakota warrior
returning from the hunt
to a woman lying in the light
of early morning, and the warrior
slips in next to her, touches her face
and says the words
that tighten her arms around him.

When I touch your face
in the half-light of early morning
I have nothing to bring you—
no talisman or wild boar, no stories,
nothing but the fall of my hand
upon your shoulders brushing away
stray threads of raven hair
making way for a small kiss
in the breath of a light breeze.

And *my breath* speaks in a language
I no longer understand,
where any word I might say
in the most inarticulate resonance
of a touch breaks and burns
like a covey of birds rising to the sun,
rising until their feathers become light
and every wingbeat sings
as I reach my arms around you
O beautiful daybreak woman.

# **HERESIES**

Such declination scorned
where none more favorable incline

fruitful hours spent in febrile contemplation
olivides and starry climes

a case-hardened promise breeched,
direct action in the heart of diffidence

Imagine the life imagined
all breakage swept

passages churn and lock, vortices,
a singularity where nothing holds

true or not—even our reproving gods
perjure themselves and yet some flaring faith

breaks through.  What calculus defines
the face in the mirror

What derivative sets limits, proving
unequal sets equal as though

no summation possible, covalent
in our lofty speech

# POETRY

*. . . The proper subject of poetry is not poetry*

There are too many squirrel poems, grandfather poems,
mothers with cancer poems, poems
of all sorts perhaps—language poems?
As if language were not there
in any poem, bad or good, mostly bad.

Someone unlocked a CD-ROM (remember those?)
containing all the poems in English not
under copyright, and said, "All in all,
there wasn't much there."

Literary art is fleeting, like today's greeting,
"Hello, how are you?" language at its worst.
Give me just a few days with a few words
and I'll be fine.

I'll be okay.  Overhead, a mother squirrel
scolds a grandfather tossing his laughing grandchild
in the air, her mother beaming.  I wonder
who has the cancer.

# FULL MEASURE

There are enough stories about light,
its persistence, its constancy, its revelations—
any concordance proves the claim.
And enough experiments: every school child
knows its speed, even that it bends,
arcing around worlds to discover
imaginary places, some place where you and I,
love, stand in its radiant warmth, my arm
around your waist, admiring a summer garden,
a quiet pond where fish rise to greet us
shaping our reflections, and those other places,
cold and uninhabited where no god lives,
and the light is heavy, its mass cumulatively
great weighing a thousand times
what the heart weighs: we've been there too.
But the storied place always returns
in a close circle of light, a lover's embrace
as if our first touch had journeyed back
following the long curvature of space;
here a dragonfly settles on your arm,
almost imperceptible, its iridescence singing:
it measures the weight of light between us.

# PERFECTION OF THE LIFE OR OF THE WORK

In the middle of a chilly night
my grandfather walked down the stairs—
his slippers clopping, his pajamas worn thin—
unlocked the front door and shuffled
down the block, a dim street lamp
guiding his footsteps.  Cops stopped,
asked him the usual questions:  name,
where he was going, where he lived.

He said he was going to work
as he had for so many lifetimes,
repeating the same ritual
as if taking communion every day
of his life.  Maybe it is the work
that keeps us going, the work
never ending, always something to do,
rest saved for another life
beyond the halo of a street lamp.

# QUARANTINE

After the Army I wanted cessation,
no contact, no connection, no voices
to respond to: my throat closed
until it labored to be used again.

I holed up in a small apartment in Philly,
a statue of Little Nell down the block
in a small park that lay between
trolley lines—a self-imposed quarantine,

a pandemic of ceaseless alone,
a hermitage blocking out the city.
I needed reflection and Mahler
though Tchaikovsky gave me uneasy sentiment.

Years before I had read the first few passages
of <u>Moby Dick</u> on a Lake Michigan Cruise,
a car ferry bound for Muskegon
then churning back to Milwaukee.

I couldn't get any farther.  Sometimes
you have to know more, so much more
before a book speaks to you.  But,
in my quarantine I picked up the novel again,

my small apartment a forecastle
to the literary world, and Ishmael's words
caused my spine to shudder and go cold,
my heart to race, beating, beating hard

as if some ancient stone, carved
as an amulet, all lore contained. I found God.
Now it is the same—secluded, no contact
with anyone save a grocery clerk every two weeks.

I talk to myself now, like the dispossessed
in large cities, walking down streets
of avoiding crowds, pontificating,
excoriating forces befuddling their lives.

My conversations too are mindless, mostly of solitude
mocking the venerable Buddhist pattern
of Withdraw and Return.  I won't return.
There is more than a life of the mind,

more than any contact can offer.
I've changed viscerally, cognitively,
jailed by a failed language.
My voice seems hollow, contained

in some fractious geode never to be split
open, no reveal, no revelation.
And, interminably, there is nothing I want to read;
sacred texts litter the floor behind me.

*June 2020*

Still, in this time of Withdrawal,
bobbing like a cork on the waves,
the current takes me
out of myself, left to my own
devices.  I search desire
for a place to Return,
pick up a text, read briefly,

know that the mind is always
in quarantine as if climbing
an escarpment, the danger of falling,
of not fulfilling the directives
of the Oversoul.  Evening shadows
darken the room to a pleasant silence,
even the room contemplative in its nature.
"We think alike," I say in commiseration,
vespers of bird song, no more meaning than that,
a further search would prove fruitless,
contained in past sojourns of thought
and correspondingly content.

*July 2021*

# INTRUDING ON THE CONVERSATION

The goatherd says, *Indeed*
*My daily thoughts since the first stupor of youth*
*Have found the path my goats' feet cannot find.*

*Better yet,* says a man still older,
*Follow the path the goats have worn,*
*Nimble on rocks and violent slopes.*

This is where we always differ:
Meditations sighted
On such foolish tasks, some silly pleasure.

Where we end is not where we set out
All distance played and lost:
We end with a stone heart, an apparition of the mind.

with apologies to Yeats
lines from *Shepherd and Goatherd*

# POEM

A body draped over a balustrade
is something of a cliché, even to the one
being draped.  Last out of body
thought: "Well, I've seen *this* before.
Been there, done that."

A cliché draped over a cliché.
How not very clever is that?

And yet the news, what satisfies our hunger,
is the same dish served nightly,
even hourly now with a myriad
of notifications flooding our phones.

Three people knifed to death
in a cathedral over a cartoon
would be the subject of a cartoon
if we understood the irony
of proliferating clichés.  And yet

We go on tirelessly mouthing, "Good morning"
to the doorman, saying, "Thank you"
to the grocery clerk, "Good night" to
our spouses, as if, as if, the repetition
of corpses on a balustrade, bloody corpses
in a cathedral, were not our daily fare.

# IRIS

Early spring in all my early years
a trip to the nursery following my mother
from bed to flowery bed, from tray to tray
of even more bountiful color, annuals
of deep purples and reds, golden yellows—
coreopsis and cock's comb, changed to
coxcomb for that most early virtue of political
correctness, filling a child's coaster wagon,
the perennial Radio Flyer, overflowing
with snap dragons, poppies, sunflowers,
foxglove and phlox:  and pansies with their faces
like Disney children looking wondrous
at the world, a sacred pilgrimage
as any to the Holy Land.

So I had some awareness of flowers,
their beauty and value to my mother
and once, in a vacant field a block away,
land undeveloped though it would be
but a short time before hammers opened
the morning as they struck 10d nails
in a melodic pattern almost like a call to prayer,
I found a waste of iris, dumped there
by someone, someone who did not need
them, did not want their wild purple
upstaging their backyards, a well-
manicured convention staged for envy
of such disciplined control.

But I knew the sensuous grandeur of iris
and returned to the field with my own red wagon
and filled it and brought them home,
a gift for my mother who took them
and with her hands and a small trowel
planted them in a large, churned space
open to the sun.

Every spring they came back fuller
than the year before, a glorious
testament, a rejection really of that off-white,
beige, or muted color fashioned
in home design magazines
of the time, the color of winter so much
desired as a reflection of spotless cleaning.
"Keep it neutral," designers said, and their
counterparts, real estate agents, looking
for a quick sale: "If one wants it off the
market, a neutral (*read bland and dull
to the senses*) palette will entice
prospective owners who can add
their own color if they so wish."
Maybe a pillow here,
a vase upon a shelf that catches
the light of afternoon, a clock
filling the open space on
an indifferent wall to remind
everyone of time and space lived
colorless, bland as meat loaf and
mashed potatoes for an evening meal.

I should have learned even then
that beautiful things are often discarded,
considered unnecessary, unwanted

like collections of family photos
found in antique shops, merely
an inconvenience, clutter in someone's life.

But the invincible color of iris, a fecund
statement to the world, lives in those years
of perennial splendor, lives in my own backyard,
a whole blanket of iris under a
spreading maple, an old elm,
returning every year promising
dark blues, luxuriant purples,
but because they live in shadow
they rage green but do not bloom,
though every spring I swear I will
transplant them, always the promise,
always the untruth of it all.

But this is what one does
attempting to do the right thing—
embracing but a college level intro
to ethical philosophy—and falling short,
pretending to do better, to have done better,
when one has merely mucked it up
in a different way from past believers,
scripture prominent on a coffee table.

I recognize myself, what I have become.

This morning, after a night's rain,
ground soft enough to dig, I stand
on my honed shovel pushing it deep
and remove a cartload of iris,
plant them in a place the sun will reach

and wait.  Blind faith, faith as an extension
of reason, it matters not.

A slap in the face to do something,
though even dreaming is solid work,
for what is beautiful is often discarded,
an inconvenient reckoning, the unwanted
an offering, a flowering, an opulent benediction.

# LAST ONE

So much talk of the other side
of this world, this universe
of starry madness, despair
of things we're still afraid of
despite the hubris, voices rich
in daylight, cowering in late hours
when words are stripped
to the bone and the marrow ripped free.

I have had good Christians tell me
they look forward to a nuclear Armageddon,
to a world consumed by drought and flame,
to Leviathan in a pestilential flood:
they would be closer— so much sooner— to God.

What to fear accounts for nothing
in this world wracked with bitter
machine noise, background to the cosmos,
and that abject look in the eyes of the defeated.

You must be thinking human, homo sapiens,
an array of mortal souls—
refugee camps, internments, monuments
blown to hell, museums gutted, displaced persons,
bodies bloated, washed up on a rocky beach—
but, instead, consider some late extinction,
knowing it is the last, years without
another the same and still hunted:
the list is long and foolish to think

of some undiscovered country
where the laws of biological physics play out,
and there is no cursing of ancient gods
spitting blood with each oath.

Scripture not yet written,
there is a new commandment:
*Rage against acceptance*, despite that look
in the knowing eyes, rage on.

You will hear otherwise (as I have so many times):
"Your anger is not healthy,"
my doctor says, explaining as she has told
her children, "The bad things of this world
exist in great proliferation. You must not
let this evil consume your life."

Dear doctor, I have had enough
sermons in my life.

By now, reader, you must be wondering,
"Where are the images? This is not
a poem, barely literary, and that abstraction
*rage*? I can't see it, modern poems need
images. Otherwise words are so
deceptive."

I know, I know, but it's just a rule
of modern aesthetics, an artistic prejudice,
a way for future literary historians
to date our work though it holds *some* truth.

Still, if I make that rage come alive,
graphic images, horrific detail, photo
realism, you'll dismiss it with disdain,
contemptuously arguing, "That is not it.
That is not what I had in mind at all."

And so I won't
though this is the final war,
war between rage and acceptance,
acceptance and rage, rage on
or quietly, on a warm summer night,
stars circling, planets dipping below the horizon,
very quietly think a way back
to a sky as bright, as beatific,
as the night you were born.

# BEEN AWHILE

It has been awhile
since I've heard swarms of music,
summer full-on with a blast
of heat that lasts into the deepest reaches
of the night.  I can reach no further,
and the song is one of repentance
for all the things I have not done.

Before the heat of morning takes hold
I note the shell of a cicada
clinging to the rough bark
of a backyard tree.  It holds
that song, yearning for return,
a strong repetitive note, a hint of remembrance,
harbinger of what music next be sung.

# EXPIATION

"It is a black widow's web,"
the exterminator says after he's
put the termites under
control.  "Spray it," he says
"before they get in your house."
It is a caution, an admonition
so much like every other,
all rules to be observed,
Janissaries to the end.

I work in the overgrown back yard,
cut back the dead from an earlier frost.
It is tiring work, and endless,
as if nothing can be left alone
to live or die on its own.

Eyes blinded with sweat,
I deadhead the roses,
something I should have done
several months ago.

I need a break and walk back
inside, the heat, the exertion,
overbearing.  I gulp water— glass
after glass— and glance down,
my work jeans covered with web
stuck harder than Velcro to the fabric
of these pants, my socks, my steel-toed shoes.

And there upon the kitchen floor
a spider, sleek and black,
a black widow?  Perhaps not;
this one is beautiful in its symmetry,
its elegant legs, long and slender,
lethal in its aesthetic.

I look at it and shudder.

What would I do if it bit,
sinking its venomous fangs
into my flesh?  Where would I go
for treatment, and would my flesh
decay around the bite
leaving necrotic lesions,
deep craters in my flesh,
until little is left of the healthy
meat?  I imagine no further than that
and bring my foot down hard,
squishing it flat.

Later, and for the long days ahead,
I think of its beauty,
how often the beautiful is terrible
in its lethality, how not even God
can save us from a petty
though sacred desire to stamp it out.

# CONTRACTUAL LIABILITY

Almost nothing happens suddenly
anymore, a lie if ever there was one,
but the streets do not ignite
as evening flows, wending like cats
released for the night.  No excitement:

The usual, the mundane and eternal sameness,
now preferred.

I light candles in a cathedral, plant a five dollar
bill in an offering jar, silence my only prayer:
Qui tacet consentit.  None of this makes any sense.
I know I don't believe in anything
except the terrible repetition of it all.

Armed zealots, terrorist groups unheard of
a mere month ago, spring up
like mushrooms in a cave;
everyone expresses surprise
thinking the job was done.

The job is never done:
a bad tooth, a freckle that gets
darker, larger, an overlooked invoice
that needs to be paid.  Or else.
Surely there is some compensation,
recompense, bounty to be gleaned
from the bountiful array.

I walk across the Danube, a lovely
evening as bridge lights reflect
upon the water.  A woman
stops me, says, "You may have me
if you wish."  I take her number from her hand,
a small piece of folded paper;
briefly our fingers touch.

I wish I could partake, but I am with
a friend and colleague who would, I'm sure,
think this wrong.  But that night,
the long days after, fill with deep regret.

She is what I need, even if it is not her,
a few small pleasures at the end, a promise,
removal for a bit, some bliss, some beauty,
a stellar departure, some small completion,
a moment's renunciation of the dark beast
that awaits, that preys, that forces
some engagement with the world.

# LADDERS

At last count I own
eight ladders,

ladders of different lengths,
different purposes:

there is the small three-step
ladder my wife uses in the kitchen.

She is short and needs a ladder
to reach the top shelves of the cabinets

where all the spices reside
that have but a seasonal purpose—

and canned goods, a jar of raspberry jam,
an amber bottle of maple syrup, needed only

when the reservoirs below run out.
A fiberglass ladder lives in the basement

easily retrieved so I may change
a bulb in the chandelier, the battery

in a smoke detector when it chirps
unmercifully the whole night long

not ever, ever, going dead during the day,
and those cobwebs, running along

the crown molding of the parlor,
removed only with impending guests,

otherwise left alone as time turns reflective.
A wooden step ladder in the attic

gives access to the flat roof that crops the gables,
the widow's walk that overlooks the city.

Extension ladders behind the garage,
perched on racks behind the canoe,

all speak to an earlier time
when climbing to paint the upstairs

windows, the Victorian trim,
were acts of importance, reminding us

to take care of the home we carved
from almost nothing.  I'm done roofing.

The ponderous wooden ladder, too heavy
for a man my age to move

with any artisan grace,
may warp and weather to gray

when left alone alongside the house,
gutters still clogged with leaves.

All these ladders beg to be climbed
as if ascending, moving upward

were with purpose no longer to be served
until a young couple, very much like ourselves

so long ago, comes to take our place,
and a small child climbs, when her parents

are distracted, watched painfully
as she ascends, despite the admonitions,

"Get down from there. You'll fall
and hurt yourself."

This young girl smiles, laughs gleefully
at the reach, the glory of her height.

# PERIPATETIC

Along the way,
often leaving landscapes
of spiritual immiseration,
I have come to visit
places where goodness
and grace fill the air,
drawn, perhaps, by the scent of the sea,
shore grass waving on the dunes,
pilings wearing gray
perched upon by seagulls and terns
waiting, waiting as always
for some scrap, perhaps a scrap
of language that fills them
with a knowledge I can only pretend
to understand as it is there
on the shifting dunes, a new message
carried along with the sojourning wind
each day in a spray of salt,
and my ancestors walked this wharf
as did yours long ago
waiting, water gazing,
watching for what appears
on the horizon, wishing to come
close, to safe harbor and then the passing,
promise broken as it is fulfilled,
and the watch, the watch never
tires even as the salt breeze wends
along the quay, the tide
leaving the gift of a sawtooth

shark's severed carapace,
the long bone with scissoring teeth,
no vertebrae, nothing but the beautiful
bleached saw, hollow sockets of its eyes,
the whiteness, the glistening beauty of whiteness,
the earth, the ocean, bleached clean;
not even the white robes of Christ
compare in the morning sun.

# RAPTURE

This morning, this morning
I am too lazy, too inept
in my rising
to put bird seed
in the feeder,
a simple task
simple, elementarily simple,
so simple minded
I believe a morning dove could do it
merely by wishing it so.

The Lauds choir,
a litany of my morning birds,
rests on my stone fence
waiting, wishing, not knowing
I no longer wake
with the passions of years past,
recognizing I could have
lived a good life had I the will,
all wonders ceased
in a contemplative stupor,
politics of the moment;
root bird or die.

Give me the moments to wake up
to savor Puccini's La Boheme or Turandot
in the background
and memory of love in the morning,
bird seed spilling generously
from my hand.

# RECIPROCAL, IN A WAY

What is there now—this late hour
come round at last— to talk about?
What precept, what pithy remark
leads the earth's arousal?

Maybe these are my last words, my last years,
the last decade, possessed by garrulous
pointed observation and curmudgeonly comment.

Why all that time spent reading, studying,
literature, history, philosophy? Do I
know anything more now than then?

Yevtushenko said it was better
to think of the beautiful woman
passing beneath one's window than to write a poem.

I remember them all, passing beneath.
And paintings— nudes by Modigliani,
Valadon, Japanese shunga,
women pleasing their priapic men.

When I was young I woke early
and walked through a nearby wood
so quiet with morning
only the rising sun made noise,
and a few vaporous clouds
hung monastery still
above the trees: with sudden ambush

an owl clattered through the leaves
and my heart sprung in my chest.

The lightness of owl, the heaviness
of the world rent open, why, so many
years later, does that owl's flight

still startle?  Is it not the wakening
knowledge of intrusion, the way
days fill the lobes with clutter?

I want so little perhaps because I give
so little.  Is it time to give things away?
Time to lie in wait for the next startle?

I read and recite psalms and creeds
but I know I'm only faking, a simple
pretend game played against oneself,

all wonders left behind, for you
perhaps to enjoy in my stead.  It is this
passing that is wondrous, this giving.

Take what you will from your own owl
startling the day open.

# WE WON THE LOTTERY

I understand the math:
I am more likely to wake
on a cold summer day
a cockroach or skink
than I am to choose all the right
numbers in a Megabucks drawing—
those numbered balls seldom
rising to the top of the tube
with any that match my ticket.

My wife often says as we stop for gas
"I've never had any luck,"
scratching the goo off
the game cards purchased every time
we pull in to fuel up.

But we <u>are</u> immensely lucky
though I don't understand the physics,
my brain capturing the nature
of the Big Bang, energy turned into matter,
but not the reverse; gamma rays
under extreme excitation
transmute to solid matter,
a wild understanding far beyond
my reach, but still

I know that matter and anti-matter
should have been born
in equal parts when all this

began and it did not, a bit more
matter than anti-matter created,
elseways everything would be annihilated,
and we would not be here,
and I would not have the exquisite pleasure
of my wife sitting beside me
as we hurtle across the galaxy.

"Aren't we lucky though," I say
as she tosses her scratch-offs on the floor,
as she searches her purse for a few dollars
more.  "We are so damned lucky
the numbers <u>don't</u> match."  Our car door
closes with a solid thunk as she runs
in to purchase another card or two.

"We are so, so lucky."

# COYOTE SANGHA

From the north, northwest
a play of light and shade;
thermals awaken,
cloud shadows snake
down and along
these canyon walls,
bare faces of rock, pine
struck at oblique angles
to the crumbling stone—
freeze and thaw a process
that cuts and rives, carves
switchbacks that change
perspective with each step.

When I break from the trail
a desert toad hops under
some brush, carpets of brown
needles cushion each step;
the mule deer just stares at my approach
then bolts into the blessing of pine,
the piety of refuge.
Everywhere else it is still:
I want a temple to magically appear
near the top of this perilous slope
almost floating in the low hanging
clouds.  I want this a sangha
or sanctuary from reason,
from a phalanx of unyielding knowledge.

Circling back, I follow a light dance
in the descent, the fluid dance of a shaman
working a cure.  I stop on an outcrop, piles
of expended .45 ACP, hundreds of shells,
evidence of an afternoon shoot.  I wonder
why he didn't bother, didn't care,
to police his brass.

Later that night, unable to calm,
I push hard on a tiring run.
A coyote's black shadow
disappears into heavy brush, cuts through
as I spin to catch him crossing the street;
the streetlamp follows his jaunt
up into the hills, the Front Range:
this is the process of withdraw and return,
the eternal grace of resurrection.
*Follow me,* he says; *the temple lies ahead
just below that blossoming moon.*

# I AM TOLD THE SKY

I am told the sky
will be a black slate
as everything moves
beyond everything

Just as now
there is no time for memory
to work upon the stars
the nights working together
receding and receding

The edge of the universe
is further
than the light can reach
further than last year's embrace

And what we know
is in that space
our ancestors left long ago
we never learned
their lives

All those stories lost
until now I tell you
I have nothing left to tell